No Limit Income

How To Make Money In A Digital Economy While You Sleep

By Michael Sloan

I0474258

Table of Contents

Introduction

We live in a bold new world. We live in a world full of money making opportunities that weren't available twenty years ago. Back in the old days, the entrepreneur was a bold and brave individual who had to take time out of his life to make money in the physical world. The times have changed, however, because we now live in a digital world. What once used to be a world full of opportunity for the entrepreneur peddling his wares on the street, now thanks to online connectivity, you can make money anywhere and at any time of the day.

We live in a world that is interconnected, truly the Internet is the city that never sleeps.

But you do sleep. How would you like to be making money while you sleep? If that sounds too good to be true, that's because many people are still living in the last century. The reality of this new century is that you can make an unlimited digital income while you sleep, as long as you're willing to put the work in. We live in a world of unlimited opportunity, but if you don't know where to look, the idea of making money online can be quite intimidating. This is why we are going to be looking at how you can take advantage of the new digital economy and make a fortune, even while you sleep.

Now then, this book is not a book about how to get rich quick, there is a lot of work that we must do in order to make that kind of money. However, if you play your cards right, you will find that the potential for unlimited income is significantly high. There will be several sections of this book, each section detailing the many different ways that you can generate income through the internet. So, are you ready to start making money online? Are you tired of working day in and day out, trading your precious time for money? If so, then this is the book for you! Let's get started.

Chapter 1: Passive Income Versus Active Income

Before we get started learning how to make money online, we must be able to differentiate between passive income and active income. Depending on your goals in life, you might be inclined to choose one income generation method, but not the other. Let's go ahead and define each one so that you have a greater understanding of the difference between the two.

Passive income.

Passive income is something that generates you small increments of money over time. The goal of passive income is to progressively create income over larger periods of time. Think of passive income as a generator. You want to put your energy and time into building the generator, but when you pull the trigger and activate it, you want the generator to run itself. There are many different kinds of passive income systems in the world. Some are insanely effective for generating money such as ad sharing, but unless you put a lot of work into them, they only generate small amounts of income. If you are looking to add extra money to your bank account over the course of a few months or a year, then you might want to consider passive income. If you are planning on making a career off of this online income, passive income might not be your best bet.

When you develop a passive income system, there will be a large amount of effort for you to initially provide. Think of passive income like a rocket. When a rocket ship first takes off, it needs an immense amount of fuel to get going. The amount of fuel necessary to fly is actually quite heavy, but as the ship goes higher into the atmosphere, it needs less and less propulsion. Eventually, the rocket reaches a place where it is in zero gravity and there is no effort required to keep it there. Passive income is exactly like that. So, don't think that you can just start working on a passive income system incrementally, you're going to have to invest a ton of energy and time upfront. The good news is, if you're willing to put energy into a passive income system and get it right the first time, once it reaches zero gravity, you are set. There is little else to do except collect income every month.

There is a danger with passive income however, there is a significant number of fraudsters and scammers out there who will try to convince you that they know how to make money online quickly and with no effort. These fake passive income systems tend to promise large amounts of money in a short amount of time with minimal investment. Don't fall for these kinds of scams, the rule of thumb is that if an income system promises extraordinary results in exchange for a minimal cash investment, it is a scam. For example, if someone tells you that you can make $200 a day for only an investment of $50, they are trying to take your money. These people are getting rich off of people they scam, not their system.

Be warned, if you are looking to develop a passive income system without spending any money, you might end up frustrated. The reality is that you will never be able to make money without spending something. It does take money to make money, but you must be wise with how you invest. You don't need a ton of money to start a passive income system, but don't expect to be able to do this well for free. There is no secret method out there that will make you a fortune for no money at all. Anyone who is promising such a thing is just trying to take advantage of you.

Active income.

An active income system is a day job. It is something where you spend a significant portion of your time in order to make money online. A lot of sales, production, services and systems are based around the idea of you investing your time into an online point of sales. If you are someone who wants to be your own boss and work for yourself, an active income system is what you want to go for. The trick to building an active income system is to focus on reducing the number of hours you work, in exchange for the amount of money that you make.

In the traditional employment system, we tend to trade our hours for dollars. You spend hours a day working for a wage. This doesn't seem very fair for you, because you are benefitting your employer with your work, not yourself. Everything that you do doesn't actually advance your income, it advances your company's income. Wouldn't it be for better for you to be able to advance your own income with the hours that you put in each day?

With an active system of income, every hour that you put into your own work will serve you and you alone. This means that you are not giving away your time, it means that you are investing your time. So, if you take the leap and start focusing on an active income system, it will take more time and energy to build and maintain than a passive system, but a passive income system will not reap the same level of reward that an active income system will. So, if you like the idea of being your own boss and the 9-5, then building an active income system is for you.

While a passive system is designed around you setting everything up and then kicking back, an active system will need you to be more involved. While it takes more energy and time, it doesn't mean that you have to be completely absorbed by your endeavor. An active system is one that could only take 10 hours a week, or if you're ambitious it could take 40 hours a week, it's up to you. But if you want to make serious money that you can live off, then you will need to use an active system.

A warning about multilevel marketing

Multilevel marketing is often called an active or a passive income generator. These things, however, are nothing more than scams designed to take your money and take advantage of you. A multilevel marketing system isn't built around being your own boss, regardless of what other people tell you. When you engage in a multilevel marketing scheme, you are just simply doing the bidding of some other organization and they are the ones who are reaping the full rewards. If you are not familiar with what a multilevel marketing scheme is, let's go ahead a look at the warning signs of one.

Traits of a Multi-Level Marketing Scheme:

You are asked to pay for their system: For example, if you have been introduced to a system that will offer you an unlimited economic opportunity, but you are required to pay a $300 fee in order to buy the materials that may be a multilevel marketing scheme. This material will do nothing but scam you.

A lot of free services are initially offered: Multilevel marketing schemes use a free service to try and pull you in. For example, one popular method for a workout multilevel marketing system is to offer free training classes.

Over time those free training classes start pushing the product, and over time that product suddenly becomes something that you are encouraged to start selling. Of course, in order to sell the product, you will need to purchase the product. This is just a scam.

You are encouraged to share with your friends: Multilevel marketing schemes are based around marketing to both your friends and family. Usually they will use your friends to try and convert you to purchase their products and get involve in their system.

There is a chain of income: Many times, multilevel marketing schemes are based around recruitment. The person who recruits you gains a percentage of the lifetime income that you make. For example, suppose you were recruited by a friend, and in your time of working for that multilevel marketing system, you earned $1000. Your friend would maybe get 10 or 20% of that. This incentivizes your friends to recruit as many people as they can, in order to make as much money as possible. The friend, however, is not making money off of selling his products, he is making money off of recruiting other people. If there is a chain of income and there is an expectation for you to make money off of other people working, you are in a multilevel marketing scheme.

Extreme enthusiasm: Sometimes a MLM system seems to be incredibly true. You will be surrounded by a lot of people who are excited. They will tell you how great it is and they will tell you how their lives have completely changed. These work from home scam systems are reliant on making you think that it's a good deal. A tremendous amount of pressure and enthusiasm is designed to make you make commit to a deal right then and there, they will try to tell you that you need to act now. They will tell you that it will change your life but the reality is that all you are doing is making other people successful.

There are no shortcuts to success, and while there are many legitimate avenues to working for yourself and making money online, don't try to accelerate your progress by jumping aboard one of these programs. A multilevel marketing scheme only serves to make the people who invented it richer. Yes, it's true that there are some people who can make money off of the system, but the reality is they often have to spend an exorbitant amount of money and they end up too deeply involved to be able to leave. These people put a strain on a lot of relationships with their friends and family. They damage these relationships and for what? For money?

Regardless of what you want to do, there is tremendous value in choosing an active or passive income system. As long as you are willing to work hard and keep an eye out for scams, you can make great money online. Let's look at some ways how.

Chapter 2: Making Your Money Work for You

One of the simplest ways that you can make money online is by taking the current amount of money that you have and investing it into something. Now, investment can be a very busy and time consuming thing, after all, the stock market has a lot of things happening and it can be somewhat confusing. We aren't a stock picking guide, but we do have some avenues for you to look at as you consider how to invest your money. These are all passive ways that you can use your current savings in order to generate more money for you over the long-term. This passive income system works best for supplementing your income or for maximizing your savings. With this system, you are using your money to generate passive income instead of using your time.

Investment income one: peer to peer lending.

In the traditional economy, lending is primarily handled through the banks. An individual goes to a bank to ask for money and they receive a loan, the loan is repaid over time. The bank charges an interest rate and receives the profits from that loan as it is paid back. But did you know that in today's digital economy, you have the ability to replace the bank? This is what's known as peer to peer lending. The legality of this depends on the state you are in, but there are several different online websites that you can use to offer up your own money to loan to others.

Websites such as Lending Club or Prosperity Market allow for you to be the one to loan your money to other individuals. You are essentially able to loan money to an individual without ever having to interact with that individual, through an online system. They are given a specific interest rate and are required to make monthly payments, the monthly payments usually go straight into your own bank account. This is an excellent way to take a large chunk of money that you have and gain residual income without doing much work.

It's important to know that using a lending system does have inherent risks. A loan can be defaulted on; it will deal damage to the person's credit score but there is no legal way for you to make money back if the loan defaults. At the same time, most of these lending websites allow for you to spread out your loan across many different people. For example, if you are to invest $5000, you could actually spread that across 25 different investment loans. That means even if one loan went bankrupt, you would only lose $200 as opposed to losing $5000 in a single sitting.

Peer to peer lending is a new, niche online market and will provide you with the ability to make as much income as upwards to 8% returns off of your investment. That means if you are to invest $10,000 in a five-year loan, over the course of the five years you would reap $4000 in profit. That is a significantly higher amount of money for doing very little. If you're looking to build up your savings, or just put money that's sitting around to good use, then you might want to consider using peer to peer lending systems.

Investment income two: dividend stocks.

In today's digital age, did you know the only thing that you need to purchase a stock is access to a stockbroker account? Did you know that most online stockbroker accounts only require a modest investment and can start you up in less than a week? In the old days, stock sales were traditionally controlled by brokers. If you wanted to invest some money into the stock market, you'd actually have to call someone up and place an order, that individual would then call someone else to place an order and eventually you'd have your stocks purchased. This was a lengthy process and required a lot of time, energy and effort. Nowadays in order to buy a stock, you just simply have to go online, find the stock that you want, order the amount that you want and then click buy. The online system will automatically allow you to purchase the stock of your choice.

The stock market can be a tumultuous, confusing and scary place for someone who doesn't know how to navigate it. We're not talking about how to invest in the stock market today, but we are talking about a specific kind of stock known as the dividend stock. A dividend stock is where a company offers a percentage of their profits to those who own the stock on an annual basis. This is an incentive to have people invest their money into the company.

For example, if you had company XYZ offer four cents per share owned, each year they would pay you equal to how many shares you owned. So, if you had 10,000 shares you would be making $400 a month a year for just owning their shares. This requires a larger amount of money to make any real money, but it's a fantastic way to increase your income over time without having to work hard.

Dividend stocks are usually quite stable as the companies are well-established. With a little bit of homework and research, you should be able to find stocks that pay good dividends and are stable. In the long run, the more money you invest in dividend stocks, the more they are going to pay off. The best part is that you can buy them on your own using only a simple brokerage account. Brokerage accounts such as Scottrade, TD America or Edward Jones allow you to purchase these stocks without the need for a professional. Please note that stocks are volatile, but if you are investing for the purpose of receiving yearly dividends, which are paid out through the quarter, then it's generally a good idea to invest in these things. Dividend stocks are liquid, meaning that you can sell them at any time, so if you have a bunch of money just sitting around in your bank account it might be a better investment to use a dividend stock.

Both of these income systems are primarily passive. They can assist you in getting some additional cash over the years. The amount of work that you need to do with either of them is relatively minimal, but then again the income potential is not high unless you have a significant amount of money to invest at the start. Over time these systems will assist you in making sufficient money that can be quickly reinvested, growing your income potential over the years. They are not fantastic ways to generate money quickly, but they are very stable methods of earning.

Chapter 3: Affiliate Marketing.

One excellent method of gaining money is through what's known as affiliate marketing. Affiliate marketing, at its core, is driving in ad traffic to a website. For example, let's suppose that you had a blog about makeup tips. These makeup tips are about all of the different kinds of makeup that are available, different ways you can use makeup and talk about the best make up deals that are currently on the market. This blog, if used properly, can actually make you money through what's known as affiliate marketing. When you are involved with an affiliate marketing plan, you are basically agreeing to host advertisements in exchange for money. Usually you get a small amount of money made from each time someone clicks on that advertisement. For example, if you had an advertisement for a company on your blog, you might make one cent per click. So, if in a single month, 1000 people visited your website and the 1000 people clicked on that link, you would make $10.

Affiliate marketing can be a mixture between passive and active income, depending on how much energy you want to put into it. There is great money to be made off of affiliate marketing, but it does require a significant amount of time at the beginning. But if you play your cards right, you should be up and running within as little as a month. If you want to learn how to affiliate market, let's look over each step.

Affiliate marketing step one: find an affiliate.

The first thing to know about affiliate marketing is that there are services that automatically assist you with providing advertisements for your website. For example, AdSense is one of the leading affiliate marketing companies in the world. These people automatically assist you with providing links setting up your system and providing banner space for ads. Some of these affiliate marketing sites are niche, and others are more open to working with just about anyone. Now there are many different types of payments that you can receive from an affiliate marketing company, so you're going to have to navigate which one you would like. The types of payments that you can receive are:

- Pay Per Click: you receive a payment each time someone clicks on a banner ad.
- Pay per lead: you receive money each time someone signs up for a newsletter or product.
- Commission: you receive money each time someone buys a product through your website link, such as if you were to link to a type of makeup through your website, you would make a small percentage off of that sale.

- Pay per post: you receive a portion of money when you have a post directly advertising for the product. You can see this most commonly on blogs where you have sponsored posts. Those individuals are making money off of those posts.

There are numerous amounts of affiliate marketing systems that exist. You have to spend some time doing sufficient research to find one that will work with you, but then again always make sure to do your homework sufficiently. Never go with an affiliate marketing site that looks too good to be true. Most places do not pay a large amount per click, but over time those clicks will add up.

Affiliate marketing step two: develop a website.

A website is necessary because that is where you're going to be putting up your advertisements for these products or services that you are promoting as an affiliate. Now, there are a lot of different approaches to developing a website, and everyone is different. Some people prefer to make their own websites, using extremely easy to use services such as SquareSpace and others prefer to hire developers to make their own websites. Hiring a developer is much more expensive than doing it yourself, but you will get a professional quality website out of the deal, so it's up to you.

The purpose of developing your own website is to house content. The reason why people visit websites is because they are interested in the content that you are providing. So, if you have something that is of interest to them, such as a makeup review website, they will be willing to check out your content. However, don't assume just because you have a website, that people are going to automatically visit. There are billions of webpages in this world, and you do not get a piece of the traffic pie just because you are existing. You are going to have to spend time learning how to directly market to people and get them to come visit your website.

There is a ton of work involved with developing your own website, first you need to figure out what your theme is going to be. Ask yourself what will make your website different. One of the most effective methods of website development is to try and fulfill a need of the market. Think of the things that you have a unique spin on. Over time, you're going to need a website that is markedly different from other people. For example, if you're going to make a gaming website, then you're going to have to figure out what makes you different from all of the other gaming websites that exist. You can't just simply assume that people are going to visit your website, because you are about gaming. It's a competitive world out there, so you're going to have to figure out what works best for you.

At the same time, you're going to need to pick a website that has room to grow. Websites do not function without continuous content, so whatever you make is going to need to be updated on a weekly, daily or monthly basis, depending on how much money and time you want to put into your work. Once you figure out what kind website you want to host, you're going to need to start filling it up with things of value in order to attract people to it.

Affiliate marketing step three: develop content.

Content can be defined as anything that provides information or value to the readers. For example, a blog review is content, as is a video on YouTube. Anything you put on your website that is designed to entertain, educate, or interest your customer base is content. Content is king. If you want to make a lot of money doing affiliate marketing, then you're going to need high-level content that continuously pulls people in. Good content pays well, because the longer someone is on your website, the better chance they have clicking your affiliate link, buying the product that you're peddling, or just sharing your links. There are a lot of things that your website depends on, but good content is priority number one.

The problem is that you are going to need to be the one who develops all of that content. Now, if you're a hobbyist who's just wanting to make a little extra money on the side, you might want to only update your blog once or twice a week. Infrequent updates mean people won't visit your website as often, meaning you'll make less money through advertising. But if you're looking to make serious money and treat this as an active system, then you need to write articles every single day. This can be extremely exhausting for people which is why you have another option at your hand. You can hire what is known as a virtual assistant to assist you with your process of writing content.

You can hire a virtual assistant through various different websites, such as UpWork, in order to do certain tasks for you. For example, a virtual assistant could write and research articles for you. Now, the mileage will vary depending on how you pay them. If you pay them the bare minimum, they most likely won't produce high quality content. At the same time, if you are making a lot of money and you need a lot of content but you don't have a lot of time, it might not be a bad idea to hire people to bulk write articles for you and then act as their editor. This will increase your potential to make income, because the more content you have, the more people will be pulled to your website. Affiliate marketing is based off of content, the more you have, the more money you'll make.

If you're very serious about making money off of affiliate marketing, then you'll want to put together your own team. This team could be a team of ghostwriters who you tap to make you brand-new articles that are high quality each and every week. This could be a costly endeavor but you will save more time than having to write each article yourself.

Affiliate marketing step four: optimize traffic.

If you followed all of the steps so far, you should have a website with good global content that is designed to please your target demographic. What's next? Do you just sit back and wait for people to come in and start clicking? Not at all! You now need to start finding traffic. Just because your website exists doesn't mean that people know that it exists. You need to be able to get your website in front of the people who will most likely revisit that website. Believe it or not, but there are a lot of bots in this world who are consistently trawling across the Internet looking at websites. These bots aren't purchasing anything and they're not clicking anything, so sometimes you might have interesting traffic that isn't actually a person, it's just a bot. This can give you the illusion that you have good traffic, when in reality you don't at all.

If you want to make money off of your website, content is only half of the equation. You need to have people consistently visiting, clicking and sharing your content. The more people who land on your website, the greater chances you have of them clicking ads, purchasing things and increasing your overall revenue. So how do we do this? It's simple, we focus on the things that optimize our traffic. There are four different things that you can do to assist you in optimizing your online traffic.

Traffic optimization tip one: SEO.

SEO stands for search engine optimization. The majority of traffic that you're going to receive that isn't targeted is going to come from search engines. A search engine is something like Google or Yahoo. These search engines are constantly sending people to relevant websites. For example, if I were to type in makeup reviews, it would bring up the most optimized makeup review websites. In other words, Google looks for the most relevant thing that it can find and then offers it to you. Search engine optimization is optimizing your website with a specific set of keywords so that Google knows exactly what your website is about. So, if you had a makeup website, you wouldn't rank very high because there are thousands of makeup websites.

What you would want to do is optimize your SEO so that your specific niche can be found. For example, if your niche is makeup reviews for Asian women, you would want to optimize it as much as you can so that when someone types in "makeup for Asian women" into Google, your website will show up in the first few pages. SEO optimization is one of the hardest things to do because Google is consistently changing its formula. There's a lot of ways for you to try and game the system but a lot of these things are unethical actions. If you're going to sincerely prepare your website to be visible online, to be found through search engines, then you are going to put a lot of energy and time into researching keywords that will optimize you for SEO. You might want to even consider hiring a service, and if you do please make sure to not skimp out. Most SEO services that are cheap will just use targeted traffic systems that will only take your money and not actually put you anywhere visible.

Traffic optimization tip two: traditional advertising.

Facebook has one of the most efficient and highly targeted advertising systems that exist in the modern world. With Facebook's unique algorithms, they are able to put your ads directly in front of the kind of person who would be interested in clicking. The downside is that these kinds of ads cost money. However, if you are able to effectively invest your money into using Facebook ads, you can significantly increase traffic to your website. If your website is of sufficient quality and has a good retainage system, something that we will talk about later, you should be able to significantly increase quality traffic over time.

The goal isn't to get 1000 people to visit your website only once, rather you want to have committed followers who are consistently going to your website. It's better to have 10 people check your website every day than it is to have

1000 people check your website once. Traditional advertising affords you the ability to get your product out in front of people, your product is the website. Facebook advertisements can be relatively cheap as well and provide all the analytics to give you the exact understanding of how effective each ad that you run is.

Traffic optimization tip three: guest blogging

One exceptional way to provide links to your website is to do what's known as guest blogging. You have two options when it comes to guest blogging. Guest blogging involves hosting someone else's content on your blog or having someone else host you on their blog. This is a mutually beneficial arrangement, because it sends traffic from your website to the host's, and it sends traffic from the host's website to you. It is usually a win-win situation. However, guest blogging can be a little difficult, if you aren't of note. This is where personal relationship comes into play. Having a good relationship and connecting to blogs that are of like mind can help you increase traffic to your website. When it comes to blogs, everyone can be friends, there is no reason to have cutthroat competition. A website that is similar to yours can be your friend, not your enemy. If you want to increase your traffic, then you might want to consider asking someone to write an article for your website as a free promotional thing. They most likely will take you up this opportunity. This will create a relationship and later on they will most likely return the favor.

Traffic optimization tip four: have a mailing list.

A mailing list can be one of the most beneficial things that you can ever develop. In fact, if you're serious about online marketing regardless of what you are doing, the mailing list is the secret weapon of any individual who is trying to make a fortune through online work. What is a mailing list? A mailing list is simply where you get someone's email. You use a website like MailChimp in order to manage your mailing list. This allows you to send updates to your client base. I cannot stress the value of the mailing list enough to you. One of the main features of the mailing list is it allows for you to send direct messages to your clients, telling them about your website, if you have new updates, new pieces of content or if you want to create a newsletter that's composed of links to your website. You can do all of this with a mailing list. If you have a product that you're planning to sell as well, then you can use the mailing list to sell that product directly to them.

There is only one major challenge with building a mailing list. That challenge is convincing people that it's worth signing up for your email services. This is a precarious situation. People need to trust that you are legitimate, you need to be able to communicate to your customer base that you will not take advantage of their emails. There are a lot of unethical practices surrounding emails these days, especially considering how many companies are willing to sell emails to third parties. Most people are very hesitant to share their email information. Secondly very few people are willing to just part with their email for no reason. They have to have something in return. And this is where a product comes into play.

One of the most common incentives that you can offer in exchange for an email is what's known as a freemium or free product. This free product will allow for you to share an e-book or some other product in exchange for their email address. This is an extremely effective model for getting email addresses. The most straightforward method is to create an e-book that is based off of what you are doing. For example, if you want to make an e-book in order to get emails for your makeup website, you might want to make an e-book about the seven different kinds of lipstick. Or you might want to talk about shopping deals and how to effectively find a makeup bargain. The decision to create an e-book is a no-brainer. You will have a far better chance of getting people to sign up for your newsletter once you have the e-book, as opposed to offering them nothing.

E-book creation doesn't have to be a big deal, it's very easy to make your e-book. If you don't have the creative acumen to make your own e-book, you do have the option of hiring someone to make an e-book for you. The e-book should be of high quality and should be designed to reward the person who signed up for your email list, but it also doesn't have to be a large book. But do not neglect the power of the email list. Once you have an email, you have a significantly higher chance of capturing your customer base interests, so make that e-book!

Once you have effectively created your own website, developed a good traffic stream and are regularly producing content, you should be raking in some amount of money. The more energy and time that you put into your work, the more money that you will make in the long run. Affiliate marketing and website optimization is no small task, the more research and homework that you are willing to do, the longer the hours you put into it, the more money that you can generate. This is primarily one of the most significant ways to actively and passively generate income.

The affiliate marketing system works as a significantly effective foundation for making money online. There are several different options that you can take that will put your income level over the top. We'll go ahead and discuss the e-book system in the next chapter. Even if you're not super interested in generating income through ad space, the principles listed here will serve as the foundation for you making money through other digital forms of sales. Ready? Let's move on.

Chapter 4: Write A Book, Get A Check

Long ago there used to be a world where only a select few people were able to create and publish books. These select few were chosen through a rigorous interviewing process required sometimes years and years of rejection before an author was able to get his book into the book stores. That era is long gone now. The gatekeepers are dead. We live in a new world, a world where you can make money through making books. How? Through publishing an e-book online!

E-books are rapidly overtaking traditional book sales. Not only are e-books overtaking traditional books, they are also blowing up in terms of popularity. Readers are now able to consume books through new markets, letting them find new writers directly online instead of having to at a retail store. This allows for the customer to find books that are more similar to his own tastes. The authors are no longer required to have to use a publisher in order to become published, with the advent of things like Amazon and iTunes, the book writer is now able to directly publish his own work at no cost to himself. This is a tremendous shift from the old era where making money through book writing was a long arduous and painful process. Back then, making money through writing took forever and the risks were extraordinarily high.

Traditional publishers require at least 10,000 copies to be sold before they can even make a profit. With online publishing the cost of distribution is insanely low, you can make a profit on your book tomorrow for no cost. This changes the entire system of writing books for money. You are now capable of writing a book and getting paid for that book without having to go through any kind of approval process!

The e-book market is more profitable than ever. Millions of dollars each year are going into e-books, and guess what? You can get in on that action! The e-book market is extremely competitive, but if you're someone who has skills with writing, then you might want to consider trying to make a killing off of the e-book market.

We won't talk about how to make a book, because that is an extremely long and arduous task so we're going to make some assumptions.

We're going to assume that you have already written a book and now you're thinking about how you can make money off of it. So how do we make money off of an already produced e-book?

The first thing to realize is that when it comes to e-book sales, you are not an author, you are a marketer. Most authors, when they first start out, don't realize that their job isn't to write a book. They don't understand that their job is to *sell* the book. You can have the highest-quality book ever written, but if you do not have good marketing skills, no one will ever hear about your book. There are millions of books published each year, some books aren't very good, but these books are well marketed and they tend to dominate the markets, regardless of quality.

The truth is, you don't have to really create the best possible work to make money in the e-book market. You just need to know how to market it to the right audience. So, that means your job, once the book has been created, is to be the world's best marketer. How do we learn to market an e-book? Well let's take a look at a few steps that can help turn you into an e-book marketing machine!

E-book marketing tip one: price aggressively.

Prices can range from a dollar to $10, or even $20. One of the first steps that you need to master when it comes to developing an e-book price strategy is to understand how much books in that field goes for. You need to know what the average purchase price is for the genre of book that you are selling. It can be extremely tempting to sell a book for $.99, but there is a danger in doing that. Many times, e-book readers don't mind paying a few dollars more, because people who read e-books tend to traditionally purchase multiple e-books throughout the year. This means that they have an allotted budget for spending on books. These are the people that you want to target, because these are the people who are willing to pay a little more for quality. A $.99 sticker will indicate that your book is worth exactly that $.99. At a gas station the average candy bar is valued at $1.24, so do you really want to sell a book for less than a Snickers bar?

When it comes to book sales, the cheapest is not always the best. So, don't immediately think that you can underprice your competition. Sometimes when you charge a low amount for your book, people will become worried that it's not actually worth a lot. Spend time on price research, make sure you're looking for other books in a similar genre and see what they're selling for. This is extremely crucial if you are going to make any money online selling books online and have a viable business. Most Amazon book sales do well between the 3 to 6-dollar range. But then again it highly depends on what genre. Nonfiction books tend to sell a little bit more than fiction books, and books that are part of a series can get away with being cheaper. If you're new to the e-book industry and you're trying to make a name for yourself, you might want to consider just simply putting your book up online for free. A free book, especially if it's the introduction to a series, can be an excellent idea, as it will build you up your reputation with people who are interested but aren't willing to purchase your works quite yet.

E-book tip two: Sell through social media.

Social media is going to be your best friend when it comes to making sales for your book. Any serious e-book author needs to have a significantly well-developed social media platform in order to be able to make sales. There are many different types of social media, so pick the one that connects you best to your audience. Twitter is a fantastic tool, as is Facebook.

The entire point of social media, however, isn't to just cold call and aggressively market to people, rather it is to connect to them and build relationships with your target audience. When it comes to making sales, having a relationship with those whom you are trying to market to increases your visibility to them. People do not want to be sold anything, rather they are looking for things that add value to their lives. When you are able to connect to someone on a relational level through the use of social media, without directly selling to them, it makes it far easier for you to be able to communicate to them about your work. This connection will help your potential customers see the value that you can add to their lives. Social media is not about tricking people into buying your stuff, rather social media is simply about doing your best to connect to a fan base and provide them with quality content.

If you are not using social media, then you are missing out on a potentially effective weapon to use in your marketing plan. What makes social media so valuable is the fact that it allows you to connect to your potential fans on a deep emotional level. What's even better is that you can do this without having to spend a significant amount of money. Organic engagement doesn't cost a dime and can allow you to hear from your readers and learn what they desire.

Many times, in social media we can see companies try to just repeatedly advertise for their products. In the process of advertising for their products, they end up just simply repeating themselves over and over again without any real attempts at fostering a human connection. This is seen as massively inauthentic and turns people off to sales. An author who consistently engages with his audience, talks to them, shares content that he didn't design, and provides value to the world around him will consistently get more sales than someone who just spams a link to their product on Twitter every three hours.

The key to social media engagement is creating and providing value. Everyone is busy, everyone has stuff to do, if you can get yourself in front of them and share things in such a way that will cause them to have a personal relationship with you as the author, all you have to do is just link them to the thing that you made.

Social media marketing is a tremendous machine and has essentially changed the way marketing works forever. If you are not up to date on Twitter, Facebook, Instagram and LinkedIn, then you are losing the war in marketing. You can make a killing off of e-books, but you are going to have to use social media in order to do so.

E-book Tip three: connect people to your website.

As we have talked about before, there is a tremendous value in having a website. More so, if you have a website that builds an email list, it will boost your capabilities to make money as an author. The reality is you will not make a serious fortune off of your first book. Very few people get so lucky as to suddenly sell several million copies of a book. The reality is each book that you release should help build a fan base that will carry you on to your next book release. One of the ways to set your next book release up for success is through using the email list.

Since you are creating e-books to sell the people, it makes far more sense for you to give away one of your books or perhaps a prequel to your books through your email newsletter system. This will allow you to directly email all of your previous customers once your new book releases. This marketing system is dirt cheap and has the highest rate of returns because those who sign up for your mailing list are interested in the products that you are offering. But in order for your fans to be able to sign up for your newsletter, you're going to need to have a website where they can find you and connect to you. It's a good idea to have links to your website within your e-book. This is easy to do and can quickly direct them towards your sales funnel!

E-book Tip four: run limited time promotions.

Everyone loves a contest, because contests allow people to receive free stuff! Giveaways are a great way to drum up attention to your website and your book! Some contest systems allow for people to get additional entries in exchange for sharing the book, liking it on Facebook or giving their email address.

Limited time price reductions are also another fantastic way to sell your book. When you have a sale, it's far easier to attract people to purchase the book than if you were to just charge a regular fee. A price reduction shows up on many different deal seeking websites and can drive traffic right towards you.

One excellent tactic is to run a sale in conjunction with the contest, that way it generates enough attention towards your product. Remember the whole point of e-book marketing is to get your product in front of people who are most likely to buy it.

One of the major benefits behind e-books is that you can make a monthly income at no cost to you. Each time you make an e-book it will generate sales, and the best part is your bookshelf stays around forever. If someone buys your book and they like it, they might start buying more books from you because they like you as an author. This means the more e-books that you produce, the greater chances of you making money in the long run. And since your shelf never erodes, fades or costs you money over time, each book written has a greater chance of catching a bite from a new customer.

If you're after a passive income system, then writing a book and then just forgetting about it is a great way to make a little bit of extra cash each month. If you want work on an active system, then you are very welcome to focus on building up your marketing skills and increasing your rate of sales each month. As you focus on increasing your sales, you can start building up loyalty and a strong retainment system.

It's important to not be discouraged when you first start out. E-book sales are not a lottery, most likely when you first get started you won't really have a lot of great numbers. It can be discouraging, especially if you're hoping to see thousands of sales in the first few weeks. E-book sales are a slow steady race, a marathon instead of a sprint. If you are able to increase your sales by 10% each month, you will see a slow snowball effect take place. Soon your income will begin to steadily increase with each passing month and you can then use that money to invest in more advertising. The beautiful thing about e-book sales is that you don't have to pay out of your own pocket to put them online. When you sell a book, Amazon takes a commission, but otherwise you aren't charged to put your books online.

But what if you aren't a talented writer? Does that mean you can't sell e-books? Not at all! There is a method of selling e-books that doesn't require you to do a single bit of writing. This method makes plenty of people money and can help increase your income over the months. This method is called hiring a ghost writer. Ghost writing is a common practice; you hire another writer to write a book for you and you get all the credit for writing it. Ghost writers work for a lump sum, they are usually paid by the word. The ghost writer's job is to write a book that will make you satisfied. You can use different websites to hire ghostwriters such as UpWork or freelancer.com. On these sites, you can post a job listing and have various people apply for it. Upon hiring the ghostwriter, you have them sign a contract that releases all of the book's rights to you, making you the legal owner of the book. This gives you permission to sell the book however you wish. Most ghostwriters make their money off of writing books, but not selling them.

If you are so inclined, you can make a small entrepreneurial business by hiring ghostwriters to write e-books and then selling their product. This removes a tremendous amount of work from your plate and increases the rate of production that you have. Now your mileage may vary depending on what kind of book you're looking to get made. Some books such as nonfiction can sell very well, as will romance, you are not always going to get the most highly skilled writer, but you can get writers who are somewhat skilled in their respective fields. Of course, the more you pay, the better quality you are going to get. Writers that you are working with on the lower end my not produce the highest quality, but it will still be enough quality for you to sell.

As always, you want to be careful when working with ghostwriters, you never want to use a disreputable one and you certainly want to make sure they're not committing plagiarism. Plagiarism can be a serious problem in the writing world and Amazon has algorithms designed to detect such a thing. If your book is suspected of plagiarism, it will be removed from Amazon's marketplace.

The use of ghostwriters will significantly increase your production capability and once you have enough products online, it's just a matter of continuously making sales. You have to learn how to time the market, and see what's in demand in order to sell certain books. It pays to be a writer in the modern era!

Chapter 5: Course Marketing

There is one excellent way to make money online. It requires a lot work, but can pay off in spades. This is what's known as course marketing. Millions of people online purchase educational courses on a regular basis. The question is, do you have some level of expertise that will assist you in creating an educational course? An online course is easily one of the most profitable methods of making money because it is selling an extremely in-demand product: information! Information sells online because people are always looking to learn!

An online course is nothing more than an educational course designed to teach a person about a subject. There are thousands of online courses, some courses teach about how to make money off of marketing, other courses teach things such as programming, history, art or countless other subjects. If you have a level of technical knowledge or an expertise in something, you might want to consider creating a course marketing system.

Course marketing can pay very well due to the price point of most of these courses. For example, a simple course on how to become a better blogger can sell for up to $300 per person. That might seem like a very pricey system but there are people out there paying those fees. Now, when it comes to coursework you cannot fake quality. You should not pretend like your course is really good if you don't have the technical acumen to educate on the subject matter. You shouldn't try to trick people into buying a subpar product.

One excellent method for course development is to make it a part of your website. Your website can be extremely valuable when it comes to long-term course marketing. For example, let's assume that you have that makeup website that we talked about earlier. You could sell a course on how to do makeup like a Hollywood star. The course could be four weeks long and each week has a two-hour long video attached to it. You could charge $100 a person and, if it's sufficiently attractive enough, people will buy it.

Now producing a course takes a lot of work, you'll need some form of camera equipment, sound equipment and you'll need to record and produce the videos. After that you'll have to edit them so that they are pleasant to watch as well. This can be a long and exhausting process, but it can very well pay you back tenfold.

The ultimate trifecta of online money making is to combine affiliate marketing, e-books and courses into one perfect website designed to generate you a ton of income each month. This type of system is used time and time again by many different affiliate marketers and guess what? They are all making money from home. They're sitting around in their underwear doing whatever they please and making money while you're busy working for the system.

When it comes to creating your own courses to make money, you'll need to be careful. There are a lot of different competitors out there, so you need to be sure that whatever course you're making is something that not only are you skilled with, but something that you are passionate about teaching to other people. Do you have a hobby that you're quite skilled at that could be taught to others? You can take that niche knowledge and turn into a course. Are you passionate about fitness or health? Those things can translate to quality courses as well. Just about anything that you can think of can be turned into coursework. The danger though, is that if you do not put in the right amount of time, effort and energy to create these courses and you don't deliver value, you could potentially end up being accused of being a scammer.

That's why if you are going to make a course then you must commit to making something that is high quality. It does no one any good if you are just faking quality. Now there are two kinds of courses that you could develop. The first course is a course that you teach people live while using an online platform. There are many different platforms for coursework, so you just need to spend some time online looking for a course hosting website that fits your needs.

How live hosting would work is that you have people pay for slots and you have a start date. That course lasts for a certain number of weeks and will require you to be online during a specific time of day. This would require you or someone you hired to teach others live during the period of that course. You'll be required to lecture and critique your students, communicate with them one-on-one and use an online platform to share information. The best part about this course system is that while it is active, it doesn't require you to do anything except work from home. A well-designed Webcam and a good microphone set up can allow you to work wonders with the students who might be all over the world. There are plenty of different websites that are willing to do the hard work of hosting the course work for you, so you don't even have to work on developing your own system. You just need to develop your own actual curriculum, find a host and set up your very first online course!

The second type of course is a self-paced course. This is great if you're trying to develop a passive income system. There is a lot of money to be made off of this passive income system because you don't have to be around to have people attend your classes. You just record all the information at one time, develop your own curriculum, and then once someone signs up, the system automatically distributes the courses to them. They are then able to take the course at their own pace. It's perfect because you are developing a product that requires little time after you have finished making it. This means you might have to put a few hundred hours into developing a good course, but once you have it made, it's there for life. You don't have to ever worry about spending time on it again.

There are a lot of different options you have when it comes to developing your own courses, and pricing can vary. Certain websites like Udemy offer specials and will help promote your courses on their own website. The average course makes about $7000 off of Udemy. If you are able to invest your time and energy into a course, and you have the expertise or at least the desire to learn the expertise, then I would strongly recommend you make some courses.

People interested in your courses will most likely come in contact with it on your website, but there is one tremendous free tool you can use to market your courses. This free tool is the podcast. Podcast have grown in massive popularity over the last few years. In fact, the audience for podcasts is now 57 million people and that is only in America. Podcasts are invaluable and they can provide you with a free avenue for marketing your courses. For example, if you were to develop a podcast that was based around the topic of whatever your course was about, you could create a weekly show that talks about things that would pull people into listen to it.

For example, if you were selling makeup and makeup courses, you could create a podcast that reviews makeup. Then, once you start building up a follower base who are listening to your free podcast, you are free to market both your books and your courses for absolutely free. This creates what's known as a sales funnel; since people are regularly listening and following your podcast, they will be more inclined to trust you. This trust is worth a fortune, but it cannot be bought. It can only be earned through serving your people faithfully. That is why if you were to create a podcast you should do so with honesty, earnestly and with a relentless commitment to quality. People can sniff out inauthenticity, if you are not willing to be authentic as you market your products, they will pick up on it.

In today's society podcasting is far easier than you might think. In order to do a podcast, all you need is a decent quality microphone, one that you can purchase for around hundred dollars or less, and some audio editing software. The most popular, cheap audio editing software is known as Audacity and Audacity is completely free. After you make the podcast, using iTunes and a server that will host your podcast episodes, you are then able to upload as many podcasts as you like.

Podcasts are a fantastic way to market any course, because it allows you to consistently provide value to people for free. Remember, the whole point of good marketing isn't tricking people into buying things, it is to provide value enough to where potential customers trust you. A good, free podcast is a great way to provide value to people and to solve a need. Of course, it takes a bit of work to get your podcast to a place where it's popular but if you think about it, if you have a podcast, a website, e-books, a strong social media presence and online courses, then you are going to be fighting the war on so many different fronts that you can't help but make money!

This will be a bunch of work at the beginning but you will find over time it gets easier and easier. As you make more money you can start hiring people to do some of these tasks for you. For example, you could even hire someone to produce and write your courses for you, instead of making them yourself. This frees you up to focus on other projects and still makes you more money in the long run. The goal is to make as many products as you can, so that as you build up your media empire, you are able to constantly be making more money. This is the true meaning of unlimited income!

Chapter 6: Etsy

If you are an artisan, or a tradesman, someone who creates trinkets or other physical items, don't worry! There's a place for you in the modern digital economy as well. You can sell your work on a website called Etsy. Etsy is a fantastic new website that allows sellers to directly sell their handmade goods. If you're someone who has craft of sorts, you can sell your stuff to people all over the world! The best part about Etsy is that you don't have to maintain the stock, because almost all Etsy products are made to order. This means that if you want to sell someone those handmade bracelets that you make, you can have a wide array of different bracelets to sell, but you don't have to create any until you get a sale. If you are handy with your work, then you can make a killing off of Etsy.

Regardless of what you are making, when you decide to start an Etsy shop, you are going to be able to make a lot of money if you are willing to put in the hard work. An Etsy shop is easy to put together, all you need to do is go to the website, sign up, make your shop and then start peddling your wares. But if you want to be successful selling on Etsy, then you need to remember these few tips.

Etsy Tip one: build a killer brand.

A good brand is always important if you're looking to establish a relationship with your buyers. This means that you should develop some kind of signature look that can quickly and easily be attributed to your handiwork. For example, if you are an artist, sticking to one style can help develop your brand. Or if you're a woodcarver using a certain kind of carving technique consistently will give you a type of signature. There are thousands of products on Etsy that are vying for people's money, but the reality is people usually don't buy products, they buy brands. If you can be aggressive in your branding strategy, you can build a loyalty with your customer base. Over time this loyalty translates to significantly more sales.

Etsy Tip two: good photography.

Etsy will have pictures of whatever product that a customer is looking at to purchase. If you have ever seen the food advertisements, you will notice that the food advertisements themselves look more delicious than the food does in real life. This is a marketing technique designed to make the item seem incredibly appealing. It is possible to make a burger look just as good as a magazine article, but it requires a certain amount of lighting, angles and adjustment. Your photography of your product should look this good. This is because people are traditionally going to buy with their eyes. If you are a craftsman who is developing a fantastic product, but you have fuzzy, or shoddy photographs then they will never really be interested in the product.

It's way better for you to make a conscious decision to have professional looking photos. Remember if you're making money off of selling a physical product through an online medium your customers are not going to be able to physically inspect it until they receive the product. This means it's primarily your job to make them feel as if they were holding the product in their hand through your photography.

Etsy Tip three: Pinterest.

There are a lot of different social media platforms that you can use to market your wares through Etsy. But of all of the social media platforms, Pinterest is one of the best. If you aren't familiar with it, Pinterest allows people to share pictures of things that they like, these are usually arts and craft type things. People share them and create their own little boards where they favorite the things that they like. With proper use of your Pinterest account, you can advertise for your work, organically raising interest in what you are crafting on your Etsy account. After you generate interest, they will start taking your own product pictures and put them up on their boards. The more circulation your product gets across Pinterest, the more traffic that goes to your Etsy shop. And more traffic translates to more sales!

Etsy Tip four: be personal.

In today's world of mass production and corporations, personality has been somewhat lost. Since the nature of Etsy is connecting buyers to a seller who is handcrafting the work and sending it to them, this allows for you to connect to your customer on an entirely different level. What this means is that you have the opportunity to interact with them in such a way that will leave them feeling loyal to you. For example, if you were going to send them a package because they have purchased a product from you, there is an opportunity to slip in some extras, write them a thank you note and express your appreciation towards them. A customer who receives good treatment from an Etsy seller has a better chance of returning to that same Etsy seller. They also have a better chance of talking about that Etsy seller to other people. Word of mouth referrals are extremely important, especially in the craft sales market.

Etsy can really pay off; it can turn a hobby into a lucrative money making system. You just need to be willing to continuously work on your marketing game. Remember, you can have the best product in the world but if you don't know how to market it, it'll never move off the shelf.

Conclusion

The world belongs to people who are self-starting these days! The potential for unlimited income is definitely a possibility, but the question is, are you willing to do the work to get rich while you sleep? Or are you just simply hoping to get rich by buying that lottery ticket? These tasks are not easy. If they were easy, everyone would be doing them. But at the same time, just because it isn't easy doesn't mean it's not worthwhile. If you're tired of being jerked around by a boss that you don't like or having only five vacation days a year, you might want to consider sucking it up and putting in the hours to get free from the system. You have a short life; do you really want to spend your precious hours making some other guy rich? You can invest in your future right now, if you make the decision to start building up your own moneymaking system using all the tools that we have given you today.

For all the schemes and scams that exist in the world today, there is no replacement for hard work. We have hopefully given you all the tools that will assist you in making as much money as you can, but there is no replacement for spending hours upon hours of doing your homework, spending time sufficiently researching and working towards the very best possible results. You can earn an unlimited income, you can earn money while you sleep; all you need to do is just roll up your sleeves and get to work!

Other great books available by Michael Sloan on Kindle, paperback and audio:

The Art of Thinking Big: How to Establish and Reach Your Goals, Be Successful and Achieve Anything You Want In Life

The Art of Public Speaking: How to Speak In Front of an Audience without Fear

The Art of Problem Solving 101: Improve Your Critical Thinking And Decision Making Skills And Learn How To Solve Problems Creatively

Positive Thinking with Action: How to Fight Back Against Negative Thought Patterns and Win at Life

Sun Tzu & Machiavelli Success and Leadership Principles: Based On the Classics the Art of War and the Prince

The Art Of Being Prolific: How To Be Ten Times More Productive With Your Day

The Fearless Mindset: The Empowering Secrets
To Living Life Without Fear And Worry

The Art of Being Ruthless: How to Be Bold, Find
Your Spine and Take Control of Your Life